A
QUESTION
OF
BALANCE

Revd G Howard Mellor MA BD
Principal of Cliff College

CLIFF COLLEGE ✝ PUBLISHING

CALVER, HOPE VALLEY, Nr SHEFFIELD S32 3XG Tel: (01246) 582321

ISBN 1 898362 18 1
© 1997 Cliff College Publishing

British Library Cataloguing in Publication Data.
A catalogue record for this book is available
from the British Library.

Cliff College Publishing, Calver, Hope Valley, Nr Sheffield S32 3XG

Printed by:

MOORLEY'S Print & Publishing
23 Park Rd., Ilkeston, Derbys DE7 5DA
Tel/Fax: (0115) 932 0643

from data supplied on disk

This paper started life as a response to an article which appeared in *Cliff Today* in the summer of 1996*. I received more mail from that article than any other I have written, there were over a hundred responses. Three were critical of the article and its forthright stance. I decided then to work at a longer paper which could be part of the ongoing debate in our Methodist Church. I apologise to those who have had to wait for it to appear but I have found it particularly difficult to arrive at the point where *A Question of Balance* has been polished to my satisfaction. The printer is now at the door and I must hand it over. I can only pray that it prompts some creative thinking and action in the life of our Methodist Church. For a new millennium we certainly need a New Methodism.

Images of Balance

We have been called to hold things in balance by the President, Revd Nigel Collinson, at the Blackpool Conference. In this paper I want to explore what that means and to try and offer a way forward. First of all let us consider the concept of Balance.

There are many images of different kinds of balance which are very useful and each have their strengths. A windsurfer needs personal balance to be able to stand upright on a moving board, holding only the sail moving the body weight and foot holds so that the dagger board cuts into the sea. The boarder needs to know how to lean and move so that the power of the wind can be used to enable them to proceed forwards.

A skater needs considerable training to be able to undertake double and triple jumps. It is balance which comes with much practice but also there has to be a sense of confidence with the materials. Certain things need to be exactly right for the skater to have proper balance. For instance no-one could skate with laces undone, or without the blade being at the right angle.

Take the image that is found in a watch or a clock. I have all kinds of clocks in my home and many of them are of a type in which precision is everything. Not just the placing of the clock on the wall, winding it up and ensuring the pendulum hangs correctly. There has to be precision in the workings, with everything precisely in place. Similarly, with a watch. Even a digital watch needs to have the connections rightly made. What I call a proper watch, like my pocket watch, has to have all its cogs etc in exactly the right place and at the right tension so that it will function properly.

Another image is a suspension bridge, where the structure uses all the known forces. It relies on gravity for the suspended roadway to be held in place, the strength of the material has to be calculated, the stresses from the weight of vehicles passing over, along with the wind have all to be considered. Such a bridge has to have the ability for sufficient movement so that it will not simply crack up and break as did some box girder bridges in the 60s and early 70s. It has however, to be substantial enough to withstand the buffeting and rain, tornado and earthquake.

A watch and a suspension bridge are good models for the kind of balance I think we need in the life of the church. In each, there has to be movement, in each there has to be precision in the way things are arranged, in each we have to be conscious of not only contemporary changes in the substances used but also in the historic reality of the world in which we work. Like the skater and sail-boarder, Christians need to develop personal balance, taking care to ensure proper use of the equipment, without which balance is impossible.

Similarly balance in the church has to face the issues of contemporary society but also to recognise the importance of the Christian heritage in which we stand. Some people may simply want to run with modern culture. At one level they are free to do that but not also to call themselves Methodist, if in fact the way they want to proceed is out of balance with the heritage of the Church and the biblical injunctions that go along with it.

Is balance possible?

The answer of course must be yes. If we take the image of a watch, then to keep the mechanism balanced and functioning does need maintenance. It will need to be cleaned, it will need to be oiled, parts may need to be changed or replaced. Similarly with the church, we know we are in need of confession and cleansing, we need to have the enabling of the Spirit to make us work, and from time to time parts of the church not only need maintenance but also need to be replaced. For balance to be achieved properly we have to name the imbalance. Take the image of an aircraft, to know whether its flight path is accurate, the pilot needs to know what would lead the plane to become unstable or unbalanced in its flight, take off or approach. Similarly, with the church we need to name the imbalance. For instance, it is not balanced in the Kingdom of God to espouse sin, to embrace injustice, to turn a blind eye to sinful action. Engagement with the kingdom of God means that we must live according to the pattern of life laid out in the scriptures. The deliberate avoidance of that or the flagrant overturning of the moral vision of the New Testament simply has to be condemned. To avoid condemnation would be to become unbalanced.

There has somehow developed within the life of the Church the idea that balance equates to acceptance. That somehow, as Christians, openness and acceptance are the key issues. Undoubtedly they are important but it does not mean that we are to suspend our critical faculties which identify the imbalance, the sin, wrong doctrine or wrong ethos.

What is it that knocks us off balance?

It, of course, depends what sort of images we are using. For the skater, it may simply be confidence; for the windsailer, it may be rough water; for a watch, it may be a defect in the mechanism. Recently, the whole of the Hope Valley has been decorated in blue and white because suddenly this rural area wanted to associate itself with Chesterfield and its football team. Part of the reason for this outburst of support was that we wanted the underdog to win. We wanted the 'our local team' to do well but when it came to face the mighty power of Middlesborough the scales were not exactly balanced, they were tilted against Chesterfield.

Evangelicals have felt in the last few decades that the scales are weighted against them. Look at the balance of evangelical scholars in our theological colleges. They have been largely absent from the full-time staff and this has been a scandal for decades. Consider also some of the senior positions in our church, not least Chairman. Many are sympathetic but the numbers of evangelicals is not high. When we reflect that Methodist heritage and people are broadly evangelical then something has gone badly wrong.

Ecclesiastical Road Rage

It is unfortunate that we can even use the phrase "road rage" which describes in graphic terms the way that drivers seek to push others out of their way or even, to try and stop the vehicle and attack the driver. I want to use this graphic image and suggest that we, in Methodism, are experiencing forms of ecclesiastical "road rage".

I see it in worship. The way that, for instance, to use an Anglican example, a choir in East Anglia, refused to sing a harvest hymn which is well used in schools, is in the BBC hymn book used in schools, and is well known to children. Moreover, they did not merely stop singing but walked out in a fit of rage. Recently I spoke at a circuit service where the Superintendent refused to sing the song chosen by a colleague "because it was not in *Hymns and Psalms*". I have to say that equally, I have known people decide that this congregation will sing a new hymn/song/chorus and I even once saw someone march up and down the church to make sure that everybody actually was singing.

I judge that all these true examples are outrageous, manipulative, forms of selfishness in which people seek to influence the way in which worship is designed. Nothing can be further from what is appropriate in the worshipping life of our churches today. It is nothing less than diabolical that congregations fall out over questions of hymnody such as this. The church needs to come to its senses and draw on the rich heritage of all our hymnody and music. Hymns and songs and meditations and silence and music should be used, in every form, in praise of God, in penitence and in the worship of his name.

There is another form of pernicious "road rage" in the life of our church, which Methodism has had to suffer in the last few years. I refer to the debate about Human Sexuality, in which a very small group of people have sought to influence the decision making processes with a very clear and deliberate intention that the church should ordain practising homosexuals. As you know, I have made my position on all of this very clear in the past, and I do not intend to embark on lengthy arguments now. The Methodist Conference at Blackpool made it quite clear that it did not want to discuss this issue, and I had the distinct impression that people welcomed what the President said, and did not want the matter discussed further.

Now, I have to say that I am very happy with that. I think the decisions of Derby now clarified at Bristol and at Blackpool, along with the statement from the President of Conference, are decisions and statements with which we can live. However, I predict there will be attempts to overturn this process, which in this paper I am referring to as ecclesiastical "road rage". It is appropriate to speak in these graphic terms because we are referring to a one issue lobby which is intent on a particular aim even in face of the church's decisions.

The Brilliantly Flawed Quadrilateral

There is a sense that the Wesleyan Quadrilateral has now seeped into the consciousness of Methodism, and indeed the Faith and Worship course which all Local Preachers take, assumes that the Quadrilateral is a recognised method to test our knowledge. It is assumed by some that Wesley himself invented this process of epistemology but in fact it was Albert Outler, who, reflecting on the works of Wesley, first wrote about it. He was building on the work of Richard Hooker, the Anglican who had indicated that we know things through scripture, tradition and reason. To this Outler added experience, meaning in particular the personal faith experience and especially in the writings of Wesley, the spiritual experience that we have.

In its more modern form the Quadrilateral is assumed to be talking about four equally weighted aspects of the way that we come to know things. Indeed, Faith and Worship speaks of it as though any one may be the primary partner in the assessment of what we know to be true (see unit 1).

I want to say that this is a flawed way of thinking about Wesley and his theology, for whom the scriptures were always the primary document. Of course he read widely **and** urged his preachers to do the same. He knew the early fathers. He devoured literature from other cultures in so far as he could in the 18th century and quoted extensively in his writings. Nevertheless, he was keen for it to be known that he was 'a man of one book'. The scriptures were the primary document and these four elements of his thinking were not equally weighted. Even though Wesley loved the heritage of the church, both in its theology and liturgy (tradition); was trained in logic and wanted to pursue arguments so that he could see them with their strengths and flaws (reason); despite the fact that he delighted in the experience of faith and of the Holy Spirit, nevertheless, nothing for him would unseat the importance of the Scriptures.

Thus in arriving at what we know to be true, experience, reason and tradition had to be tempered on the anvil of scripture. If scripture commanded something, then Wesley understood that he needed to undertake it. If scripture forbade something, then that was to be avoided. In more recent years the Wesleyan

Quadrilateral has become a banner behind which people have been able to lay to one side the clear teaching of the scripture. This is achieved only if the four elements are equally weighted and any one can be dominant. This version of the Quadrilateral allows the scriptures to be ignored. Similarly, the use of experience as dominant suggests that if I feel something to be **true** or right, then it will be OK for me to pursue it, even though the scripture may forbid it.

Keeping a Sharp Focus

Methodism has suffered immensely in these last few years from the attempt at restructuring. There are now people of immense ability who, frankly, are out of power and unsure what their job should be. This is a tragic waste in a church which needs to engage and harness all the gifts, graces and abilities available to it. Perhaps more importantly, the church has focused on restructuring and pretended it is a mission activity. It must be clear to us that organisations in decline, of any kind, focus on structures rather than their purpose. It is an experience which is chartered in management and nationhood, as well as in the church. The worst thing that can now happen is that we focus even more on structures.

My great worry is that the bilateral talks between Methodists and Anglicans will take up the time and energies of people who now ought to be engaged in mission and who instead, engage on a pilgrimage which is going up a cul de sac. Of course, we are called to be one, and indeed, in Christ we are one. But if we spend the next decade (for that is what it would take) looking at schemes for union, as we did in the 1960s and as we did with the ten propositions, then we shall waste the energies of our churches and create anxieties among the members. The idea of uniting the structures of Methodism and Anglicanism will not create one church, it might create three and will probably encourage more. There will be Methodists who do not want that, there would be Anglicans that would not hear of it, and others who will greet it eagerly. In the midst of all that, the missionary opportunities at the turn of the millennium will be lost.

Of course, we need to recognise the ordained ministers of each other's denomination and to recognise each other's members. We have the sheer foolishness here at Cliff that if I turn left to Baslow, there I may preside at communion because it is a Local Ecumenical Project. If I turn right and go to Calver, I may not, because it is not. Yet I have worked together well with the present vicar and his four predecessors. All kinds of possibilities may open up if there could be proper interaction between us. Certainly we need that, but we do not need a whole new structure to make it happen, simply proper recognition. Moreover, we would be better not just to talk with the Anglicans, and the attempt to do so is ill judged. I wonder whether it is driven more by people who wanted it in the 60s, and now, coming to the end of their ministry are vainly trying again. The CCBI and their *Called to be One* would be a much better format to follow, where we talk to all the denominations in the country, and settle the things that should be corrected right across the board.

The key issue for the church is mission. That should be the sharp focus of our thinking and planning. It should be to mission issues and training that the church commits its resources. Any attempt to subvert the sharp focus of mission must be resisted for it would knock us off balance.

What then shall we do?

The worst thing which could happen is that we assume the image of balance is like a tug of war. In such an event, one **tries** to ensure that at the end of the line are heavyweights prepared to get stuck in and dug in. We must however at all times be positive in our outlook for we need a church which is moving forward in faith and worship, truth and love. I suggest we consider seriously the following:-

Classical Christianity

We need to have firm faith in what I have begun to call Classical Christianity. By this I mean a statement of the orthodox faith, which Methodism as an evangelical denomination holds to be true, and by which it guides its life. The scriptures, the creeds, the heritage of the Christian church including Methodism help us to face forwards into fascinating opportunities at the turn of a new millennium. To adhere to Classical Christianity is not a way of looking backwards but a way of standing on what came before so that we can look forward with both wisdom and confidence. It is a place of and for balance.

Cleansing the Temple

The story of the cursing of the fig tree has always been for me a really difficult passage. Why would Jesus curse a fig **tree** because it didn't have any fruit when Mark tells us he understood this was not the season for fig trees to have fruit? Why place this event next to the cleansing of the Temple. (Mark 11:11-25)

There is a very intriguing kind of change in the way that Jesus deals with his disciples in this passage and in the cleansing of the temple. For three years the disciples have participated and engaged with Jesus in his work. He has healed, they have healed; he has proclaimed, they have proclaimed; he has been engaged in good works, they have been doing good works; but now they observe (verse 14).

It is Jesus that cleanses the temple, he alone. He does not invite the disciples to join him, nor does he instruct them to cleanse the temple in future. Indeed, following Pentecost we know they proclaim and pray for healing and do good works but they do not cleanse the temple. Rather they engage in worship in the area of the temple courtyard know as Solomon's Portico. Cleansing the temple is Jesus' work and we must leave it to him.

Why then the fig tree? This is, I think, a dramatic parable that Jesus gives his disciples. The instruction to them is not to go around cursing trees and bushes, nor indeed other people. The instruction to them is to 'have faith in God' (verse 22). It is his instruction to us that we should forgive and therefore receive forgiveness. The instruction to faith is even stronger in the Greek text than we have it in our English translations. Have faith in God is actually in the genitive singular and therefore should properly be translated 'have faith of God'. Not only have we not to be active in cleansing the temple, we have also to be people who receive faith so that we can have faith.

There is sometimes a desire in me to **run** headlong into the temple courtyard of the Methodist Church and its decision making bodies and start to overturn tables and cast out those who do not honour the word of God and his purposes for us. I call it a temptation because I do not see in this passage the instruction of Jesus that we should do what he did. The task of the disciple in this passage is not to imitate the overturning of tables but to have faith. It would be easier to overturn tables and physically remove people, but it is harder to have faith, and that is what Jesus calls his disciples to receive.

There are times when, frankly, I would like to take some people by the scruff of the neck and throw them out of the church. There are others whose life, ethos, manipulation and deceitful dealings make me extremely angry. Jesus in this passage says leave it to him. He will win the day and we need to have the long perspective of history to see that is what actually happens.

Finally

How then should evangelicals proceed if they are to maintain balance in the life of the church? There is, as I have said already, importance in knowing where imbalance is to be found and for identifying those factors which would lead us to be unbalanced in our thinking and practice.

We have to identify the positive things and make sure they are placed before the Church. If an evangelical grouping chose simply to speak on one issue, then it would be rightly criticized within the life of the church. Balance suggests a broad spectrum, a readiness to think on a wide canvas, to see the whole picture.

My commitment is to stay, to have faith and to work diligently in the service of Christ's mission in the world. In all of this I am guided like Wesley by reason, experience and tradition under the rule of the Scriptures. I pray that many others in the Methodist church will likewise pray and work. I believe at that point we would be balanced.

METHODISM - MAKE OR BREAK?

Methodism is at a very significant point in its history. It really is make or break and it gives me no pleasure to write in this way.

Membership

Everyone will know that the membership figures of the church are awful. However you read them, the church is in steep decline and if you work out the projection far enough ahead, it is terminal.

For many years now, when faced with the membership returns, we have always managed to find some small crumb of comfort. We have focused on that and have been missing the point which is that unless our churches bring people to Christ and make disciples then the decline will continue. However, the focus on numbers, whilst it is important, may mean that we miss some very significant points.

Doctrinal Amnesia

Methodism stands in the heritage of evangelical churches that have grown up since the reformation. The church in its founding documents, reaffirmed in the uniting of Methodism in 1932, looks to the scriptures, the historic creeds and the Wesleyan legacy as being a touchstone for doctrine and practice. Above all, we look to the scriptures as the supreme guide in faith and practice.

Recently the Methodist Church has had a corporate loss of memory. It seems as though the importance of the scriptures and the received heritage of the church down the ages means very little. Unless, there is a reawakening to our doctrinal heritage, then not only will Methodism die, frankly it will deserve to die.

We need to regain our Wesleyan heritage, which places our church centrally in a British protestant tradition and gives us the flexibility to work with so many other Christians of other traditions.

Ethical Issues

There are vexed questions on ethical issues which are before the church at the moment. The inability of the church to decide in a clear way the basis of the biblical material is a consequence of its doctrinal amnesia. The debate about homosexuality in the life of the church shows the moral bankruptcy to which it has stooped. There are also issues about Christian marriage and the implications for new services which also need our attention.

Evangelism

The Decade of Evangelism set off with such high hopes and in many places it is true, especially where there has been an ecumenical response, that mission and evangelism have been extremely effective. For instance, in Plymouth and Llandudno and Cardiff there have been very creative responses. However, so much more needs to be done and the Decade of Evangelism is losing its profile and with it churches are thinking less and less about evangelism and mission. If this is an accurate commentary on what is happening in the church today, then it is immensely serious. Unless we are proclaiming the gospel and winning people to faith, then inevitably the church will be in decline.

Health

If Methodism were a patient and the doctor was giving the above kind of prognosis, we would be left to wonder whether the patient were terminally ill.

The reader must understand that I am above all an optimist and therefore I shall say that there is a way out. For twenty four years now I have committed myself to the reform of the church from within. I still feel highly committed to this process but I do not have an idolatrous commitment to this or any other denomination.

The way forward that I see is the need to face up to the fact that God raised up Methodism for a task which is not yet completed, there is a job to be done, a God to worship, a Lord to follow, and a world to win. God has provided us with the resources of his Holy Spirit to enable us to undertake this. There are many places in Methodism where there is sound doctrine, lively worship, nurture of discipleship, caring for the community and growth of the church.

This is no easy way out for Methodism. We must call people back to classical Christianity, move forward and reawaken the vision of people called Methodist raised up to spread scriptural holiness throughout the land. This is no trite "back to basics" panacea but a call for a creative response of faithful discipleship in a needy world. It is a call which recognizes that for our Church to move forward in the power of God's Spirit then we will need to honour both God's word in our decision making, and God's pattern for our lives. I wonder if we will?

In all of this you count and you matter. You can make your views known by speaking up in meetings, writing to national leaders, being at the meeting when decisions are made, praying for those who have that responsibility. I have confidence that when the people of God make their views known then Methodism will return to the right paths. Make sure your views are heard.